BOA
EDITIONS
LIMITED

American Children

American Children

Poems by

JIM SIMMERMAN

AMERICAN POETS CONTINUUM SERIES, NO. 91

BOA Editions, Ltd ⁓ Rochester, NY ⁓ 2005

First Edition
05 06 07 08   7 6 5 4 3 2 1

Publications by BOA Editions, Ltd.—
a not-for-profit corporation under section 501 (c) (3)
of the United States Internal Revenue Code—
are made possible with the assistance of grants from
the Literature Program of the New York State Council on the Arts;
the Literature Program of the National Endowment for the Arts;
the Sonia Raiziss Giop Charitable Foundation; the Lannan Foundation;
the Mary S. Mulligan Charitable Trust; the County of Monroe, NY;
the Rochester Area Community Foundation;
the Elizabeth F. Cheney Foundation; the Ames-Amzalak Memorial Trust
in memory of Henry Ames, Semon Amzalak and Dan Amzalak;
the Chadwick-Loher Foundation in honor of Charles Simic and Ray Gonzalez;
the Steeple-Jack Fund; the Chesonis Family Foundation; the CIRE Foundation,
as well as contributions from many individuals nationwide.

See Colophon on page 96 for special individual acknowledgments.

Cover Design: Lisa Mauro
Cover Art: "angel 2 graphite drawing" by Lucinda Storms
Interior Design and Composition: Richard Foerster
Manufacturing: United Graphics, Inc., Lithographers
BOA Logo: Mirko

Library of Congress Cataloging-in-Publication Data

Simmerman, Jim, 1952–
    American children / Jim Simmerman.— 1st American pbk. ed.
        p. cm.
    ISBN 1–929918–64–X (pbk. : alk. paper)
    I. Title.

PS3569.I4726A83 2005
811'.54—dc22

2004028553

BOA Editions, Ltd.
Thom Ward, Editor
David Oliveiri, Chair
A. Poulin, Jr., President & Founder (1938–1996)
260 East Avenue, Rochester, NY 14604
www.boaeditions.org

NATIONAL
ENDOWMENT
FOR THE ARTS

State of the Arts

NYSCA

in memory of Bryan Short—
scholar, mentor, and friend

CONTENTS

Monte Vista

. . . One man could not understand me because I was saying simple things; it seemed to him that nothing was being said. I was saying: there is a mountain. . . .

—George Oppen, "Route"

Monte Vista

I like how the "Specials" board is blank, blank, blank,
like a highlights film of the collective lives
of the four or five *fuck that*, rat-gray,

grease-engraved faces hovering like slowly
deflating helium balloons above
the bar. What's more, I like that it's black, black, black:

could be a Nam memorial plaque. Could be
a certificate of appreciation
from Oblivion itself. Takes you back,

as they say and, hey, dig: now it's '69
and I'm getting very drunk, drunk, drunk
for the very first time in the basement

recroom of someone's parents' *housing*,
Westover Air Force Base, Chicopee, Mass.,
Strategic Air Command, since picketed,

since closed, and where, if you had long hair
you were banned, banned, banned from the BX, Teentown,
movie show and, so, evenings, cruised the streets

or prowled the fence or hunkered any
unhassleable place you could hide
with other *dependents* depending on

nothing but a good chewing out or smack
when they got home—that and, eventually,
the draft. . . . Oppen: *You must try to put yourself*

into those times. And I do: draft and shot
(Bud, rye) and now it's Hendrix, Joplin, Sly,
Nancy Noone and I hugging and hugging

and we cry, cry, cry because Andy
Wezlowski is drafted, Al the Pal Chapin
is drafted, Gary Mazlak's expelled

from home and dying basketballs basketball
-orange on the graveyard shift at Spaldings
in Holyoke across the bridge. Ronnie

Robinson is dropping out and that flat
-picker up from Arkansas (why can't I
remember his name?) who turned us on

to The Band's "The Weight"—what about him?
Oppen again: *War, and the news / is war.*
And my old man's unaccompanied tour

of duty to Guam to load bombs means
my mom and brother and I are gone, gone, gone
in a month to St. Louis where I know

no one and don't want to go and, so, what
else Nancy and I are doing on the floor
on our knees with our wet faces smeared

together and the room tripping out
around us like a Dead light show is good-bye. . . .
'Nother draft, 'nother rye. And when the guy

at the end of the bar starts trotting out post
-mortems for the Cartwrights from "Bonanza"
(*they're all dead now*, he says, *so you know*

there had to be something, like, unlucky
or evil connected to that show)
I want to go, *What about Hop Sing. . . ?*

Which makes me think of dancing, music; and Truth,
Nirvana, Sunlight Pipe, and Rainy Day
Blues Band were the names of bands we played in.

Oppen: *Draft animals, beasts for slaughter.*
What was his name? And what was the weight
he bore across Pacific water and

into that bitter, burning country?—maybe
gazing vaguely toward some far mountain
where the bones of the holy dead are

supposedly buried; humping point and humming
to himself, maybe, "Tears of Rage" or
"I Shall Be Released". . . . I remember

how we used to greet each other with a V
made of the first two fingers, transposing
victory to the key of peace; used to

do this hand-jive thing to "Susie Q" and
at such times the world seemed, briefly, a kind
of Ponderosa of possibility. . . .

As when, stoned on our own goofiness,
we played at Chappy's Pizza and Grinders
(off-base, where we were let be) with our flatware

the tables, glasses, plates, and condiments
turned percussion instruments to the jukebox
playing Donovan: *First there is a mountain.* . . .

Oppen: *We have chosen the meaning /
of being numerous.* And I'm dreaming,
dreaming, dreaming again, as I sometimes do

drinking alone in the gauzy blue neon
of the Hotel Monte Vista basement bar,
of a distant city where the war

is over and each of us is commissioned
to return—more cynical maybe,
more furrowed by time or failure or rage but

each of us returns. And before they call
roll, I want to be able to gaze into
each face and say, *Hey, do you remember. . . ?*

Even if it's mining a mountain
with a bar straw, even if it's nothing
special, I do.

        Shawn.

                Shawn was his name.

Trails

Some trails are happy ones,
Others are blue.

—Dale Evans (lyrics), "Happy Trails"

Out There

I know where I'm going.
And it's not out there.

Where things happen and
happen and why aren't they

somebody's fault? I can
see from in here, between

the slats of the blind,
what I need to.

I can see a white truck
parked like a dog

waiting for a walk.
I can see a mailbox

with its tongue out
like communion.

I can see the mountain
I can no longer climb

beyond the ordinary,
durable pines, their spines

stiff and barked against
whatever spark wants

to burn its way inside,
and in this place what

flame or face again
shall touch me?

THE ETERNAL CITY

Sometimes I picture your face on money.

But this isn't Rome, where they know
what money's worth, which is almost

the paper it's printed on (a kind of art),

and where I stared what seemed eternity
into a guidebook, lost, side-skipping

pigeon paste, motorbikes, and swarms

of gypsy tykes excavating the ruins
of tourists' pockets, until I stumbled

onto the Temple of the Golden Arches—

McDonald's!—and across the piazza,
the Pantheon. . . . Inside, third niche left,

alone a moment with the *Ossa et cineres*

of Raphael, I thought of you; "put it *all*
in the poem" was your advice so, okay,

here you are!—among the camcorders,

cell phones, retired gods, and a pair of
kings—rumpled, broke, and amused

as you were the Green Mountain morning

you asked: among us who was writing
for posterity?, and one of us knew. Bill,

I haven't paid you your due, but need

another favor: could you please undie
so I can buy you the glass of good

rosso in the Eternal City I owe you?

William Matthews, poet and teacher (1942–1997)

NEVERLAND

I'm putting Death in this poem
to give it a little perspective—
in the way that, photographing
a mountain or lake or
Grand Canyon, one asks
a stranger (preferably
wearing a Beatles T-shirt
or harlequin hat) to pose on the lip
of the rim (in the case of a Canyon)
like a speech act.
Only the opposite: a kind
of jujitsu
like a movie
screened on a toenail
or a drug you don't like
you drop by way of making
drug-free taste
really good!
Death's here merely to illustrate
how tiny the poem is,
and flawed and insignificant:
a fly turd on a doily
in the mansion of language
if you think about it,
which is one of the things
brains do and whoever's
doesn't is hereby consigned
to the remainders table
in the bargain basement
of Oblivion,
Inc.'s Five and Dime.
Risible Reader:
let me be plain.
I said poem
but mean life.

Want your wings embroidered?
Ask Death
smoking a cigarette
over there,
mum at the border.

MAN IN THE MOON

In one dream the door thumps
and a man stands there
like a lost clock.
He's wearing some
kind of black coat
and a hat pulled so low
the shadow of it
cuts his face in half.
He's got two hands though
and stretched between them,
like a cat's cradle
or constellation, a map.
I can hear metal
snicking somewhere
deep inside the coat:
maybe a lot of loose change
wearing the faces
of crazy ladies on one side,
dead babies on the other;
maybe just pop caps, nails,
and broken machinery—
I don't know.
I'm trying to get from here
to here, says the man and draws
a finger across the map
like he's gutting a fish.
This takes years.
You can't get here
from here, I say back,
and anyway don't I know you
from someplace sundry
tires, trash, and scraps
of clothes wash up
along the river bank
and ice spits in your eyes

all winter long and didn't
we have us a time
at that dance?
You must be
mistaking me for someone
the moon dreamed up,
says the man, one night
it was so blue
it like to washed away
on the floodtide
of its own light.
You don't know beans
about dreams, I say.
He folds the map up
small as a gnat.
It's snatched by the wind
that moans through the night,
stealing its little ones back.

IF WISHES WERE HORSES

there would be a ranch called Night
Sky or Sleepy-head and a bay
with a white blaze called Sloop,
and another, a roan seventeen
hands high, called Bottom Dollar,
and wouldn't they fly
like flame licks before first light
when the wind kicks up and clouds
are kites cut loose in the dark.
There would be a river, some cool
water like a vein of silver
dimpled with trout, shivering
beneath stars innumerable
and faint as faces
forgotten by children drifting
into a dreaming deep as a heart.
The river would be called Heart,
and there would be a prairie
called Endless, shaking
out its rope of dusty miles
burled with shadows,
bunchgrass, sagebrush,
and a shape in the distance
like smoke or something lost.
The shape would be Nameless,
and the horses, the roan
and the bay, with their lips
stripped away from their teeth
like death masks and ears
ironed flat, would stop,
and nose the wind,
and nicker, their withers
trembling like spider lace.
And the shape would nicker back.

Wherever She Goes

I can still hear the lights going out
in your voice, can still feel the clutch

of us slipping. . . . I've been tripping
lately maybe too much on the wrong

turns we make nearly daily and mainly
how easy to get so stuck on some one

-way street we never arrive at where
we meant to go. So, here's the thing:

If I tattoo a ring of Celtic knots
to the third finger of my left hand

(do I linger at all in the wings
of your thoughts?), would you care?

If I ride a cockhorse to Banbury Cross
(it's a long, long ride), are you there?

LEASH

Here's where I go wrong:
I'm supposed to be walking the dog
but instead I'm thinking
about how, in the absence
of reliable information
regarding the existence of God
(that four-dimensional
conspiracy theory?),
I'm supposed to conduct my life.
And how I'm further
supposed to be cleaning
pine cones and needles
from the rain gutters
before it snows
but instead I'm digging deeper
into how hard it must be,
I mean *really* hard,
to tell someone you
really loved a lot a long time
and maybe still do
in other words but
no uncertain terms: *dismissed*
forever; vamoose.
And while thinking about it
makes it hurt a little more
in one way,
but a little less in another,
I should be installing
The Flusher Fixer®
Flapper, Drain Seat, & Timing Cup
in the toilet tank.
I should be inspecting the hoses,
belts, and fluids
on the Honda and the Harley
and maybe changing

what I said about love before
to something more lyrical
and, in fact, factual
but that's not how it feels. . . .
What I really need to do
is something soon
about the crack
in the foundation but
I can't stop wondering
who it is leaving
those hang-ups
on the answering machine
(God?, you?) when I'm away
and when I do
reach for the leash
and grab the flashlight
instead, it might be
a metaphor for what
I'm too slow
to know although
the dog barks:
which is where I go
right.

HATING THE DOG

It's not the dog's fault.
Nor the hairs in the butter
like filaments
of discouragement.
It's not the sofa
clawed to shreds
like all your dreams
when you wake
in the dark, alone,
every morning
to mop the tile,
and feed the boy,
and drive yourself
to work again.
Isn't it just life
shedding its shag
of miscues and failings
you're fretting over?
And isn't it just,
as a mother might say,
a crying shame?
No, it's more
a feeling falling
down on all fours
to the floor and howling,
just howling,
like a dog forever
on the wrong side
of a door.
And it's more, almost,
than you can bear.
Listen, pet: it's not lost
opportunity, or indignity,
or the collection
agency you hear knocking

round this morning. No,
it's just the dog
and the boy
roughhousing the house
to shambles again.
What's a mother, when
the world runs mad, to do?
Don't hate the dog.
It's boys grow into men.

Happy Trails

If it weren't for Bandit,
I'd put a bullet in my skull.
That and the fact that
I don't have a bullet.
Bullet, you'll recall, was
the name of the dog of
Roy Rogers and must be
dead a long time now,
buried somewhere on
the lone *prayer-ee*. Ditto
Roy, King of the Cowboys
(that bovine aristocracy),
who always found, somehow,
something to sing or yodel
about and, I read recently,
Dale Evans, Queen of
the West. Roy's horse's
name was Trigger (was it
happy?), and so I figure:
a couple of cats called
Smith & Wesson, maybe
Uzi, the parakeet—
a petting zoo of artillery
and, Buckaroos, it's true
it's deep cowpie in them
there hills but—okay, I
admit it—not so bad to be
alive where, any minute,
apple blossoms could spill
like silver from the stage
-coach of Heaven itself
onto these trails I'm limping
with Bandit and thinking of
you *until we meet again.*

Road Music

No one
to witness

and adjust, no one to drive the car

—William Carlos Williams, "To Elsie"

ROAD MUSIC

There could be a dog
off-leash.

There could be a bike.

There could be a kid
chasing after a soccer ball.

There could be a car.

There could be a click
in the chest.

There could be elk
in the trees.

There could be a car.

There could be a bottle
and a bottle and a bottle
and so on and

there could be a car.

There could be a shiver
in the steering.

There could be a bubble

in the brain.

There could be boxes of
belongings
stacked in a garage

and someone you won't be
running into

anymore. . . .

⊷⊷

There could be a pig
squeal of brakes,

stench of burnt rubber,

skid marks on asphalt
like soot smeared

under a sharpshooter's eyes.

There could be a car.

There could be a telephone pole,
a double yellow line.

There could be a car.

There could be a bridge
and the black ice
a bridge wears

like spandex and what
floats under the bridge

you don't want to see. . . .

⊷⊷

There could be a car

and there could be
anyone in it: you or me
or the three mangled angels

assigned to forge elegies
in the blacksmith shop
of the ear. Listen.

What do you hear?

A car backfiring
in the distance
like a rimshot?

A siren moaning
on the outskirts
of sleep?

Maybe the zither
of hangers undressed
of their shirts and trousers?

Then the ratchety music
packing tape makes
laying its little road. . . .

～～

There could be the idea
of a car and you wouldn't
be able to pass it.

There could be the memory
of a car and it

would tailgate
with its hi-beams lit.

There could be the absence
of a car and so
you'd have to imagine:

wind-brush on crushed
metal, impossible
jigsaw puzzle of glass and

there, in the ditch weed,
look, a boot

twisted at the ankle. . . .

≈≈

There could be a car

and there could be an elephants'
graveyard of cars and

you could go there,
any night,
with a hammer and a crowbar

and try to make them sing. . . .

≈≈

Or try to make a poem
about a car
and you could revise

the poem. . . .

≈≈

I wish I could get into the car
a poem, that brief
embarrassment to silence. . . .

In a poem,
the car could stop.

a set for Josh Maust (1978–1999)

≫◈≪

Formal Disorders

*So you see how much effort a man will make
and trouble he will invent to guard and defend
himself from the boredom of peace of mind.*

—William Faulkner, *The Town*

SHATTER

He loves the speed, the light breaking
off the windshield like luscious diamonds.
He loves the crimes night commits

and the way he sits like an explosion
upon this planet he's landed on and his hand
keeps shaking its gratitude. The light

changes green-yellow-red and he's not
stopping, he's moving too fast, out-of-it,
run in night's black stocking, then

he's walking: step, step. He's crawling
somewhere inside himself and zipping up
the scars, staying put, there, where the light's

not knocking around like a cop and he
wants it to stop: that *thing* that feels
like a wing ripped from a nightmare he can't

fly out of over and over and he is *so*
sober, so hi-beamed and red-lined and
wants the eyes of light to split.

Then they do. Then night cracks its.

PAIN

It's an amusement park for the unamused.
First, they put the screws in excruciating.
Then, they make it bearable. The terrible

thing, of course, is not the pain itself but
the fact that it grows, so quickly, boring. . . .
Think of St. Andrew, not nailed, but lashed

to a cross, that his suffering might be pro
-longed. For two days he hung around, not
only breathing but preaching, ceaselessly,

to a crowd which, predictably, grew
so prickly and unimpressed it threatened
violence unless he was let loose. So what

did Andrew do? *Having preached enough,*
and to die quickly, prayed that his limbs
would be paralyzed so that he could not be

cut down. . . . So that the pain (they *are,*
he *can't,* for near four hundred years so
far as painted by Caravaggio) bears you.

❧❧

PARANOID

Most people think others think of them
what they think of others. You think.
Hence: bodacious rinky-dink. Hence:

pernicious winks exchanged in the 18th
century court intrigue the brain writes
the libretto to. Powdered wigs galore

and who's that at the end of the hall,
in the bustier, whispering into the ear
of the future? Why, it's your mother!

Hence: Freud, Austria, someone's offed
the Archduke and you're suspected of
suspecting others suspect everything

you suspect they suspect of you. Too,
there's that muttering walls do plus
the way things rearrange themselves,

nearly imperceptibly, on shelves
in the dark. Not to mention the park
where dogs deliberately mispronounce

your name. Ditto the evidence—hair,
fiber, detritus of fingerprints—
the drain keeps collecting for the case

to be made against you at a later date.
You know your detractors script,
routinely, your disasters. You know

which episodes of TV shows are sly
mockeries of your dreams. Seems strange
as the stranger so head-in-the-game

he's framed in every mirror like a clue. . . .

THE ZERO ON THE ANSWERING MACHINE

Back when I *drank*, I didn't give a fuck,
or, if I did, did something dramatic
and, not infrequently, final. I don't know

if you can relate. I don't know if
you've ever stared into the red-rimmed eye,
the digital naught and sum of your life

and said: nothing. And said it too late.
October, with its O like *over*,
and the cold rain that has fallen steadily

all morning seems, somehow, to have entered
this poem. How do the wrens, those dun paupers,
abide? Back *when*, huddled inside the birdhouse

of the bottle, I wanted to *feel* nothing.
What I felt, instead, was the feeling
of feeling nothing—and felt it acutely;

all my dull remorses sharpening their knives.
It was, then, less revelatory than bemusing:
the abrupt flare of a light bulb above the head

of a light bulb. . . . Such was my cartoon.
Whatever I said bled from my mouth
like road kill in the talons of quotation marks—

so much dictation I never raised my head
from the page to see, above me, the sleek
migrations; nor the bleak, swollen gape

of the sky opening and opening
and how to close it, now, I don't know.
If you can relate, you may have a date

with your own extinctions. I hope you arrive
discreetly. I hope you retrieve the message
I left: *Long time. No see. Meet me?*

Jittery

Nancy takes me to a coffee shop called "Jitters"
which is, I'm thinking, like naming a bar "Drunk":
what you get when you get too much of what it is

they've got to give you—though that's just me
of course, going off. I'm feeling kind of drunk
on talk and too much coffee and Nancy's laughing

easy like she maybe thinks: *okay*. Me, I mean,
though I'm reading into things of course—
talk, laughter—speed-reading into things

what with all the coffee and little sleep
I'm running on of late. Things, their course,
have not been great though I'm feeling not

unhappy to be alive and not asleep and here
with Nancy blabbing out my life like some black
and white Karl Malden movie tough guy grateful

to finally confess and yes I'll obsess on
splitting that infinitive since Nancy knows
syntax (*"syn-*, together + *tassein*, to arrange");

Nancy knows yoga, Neruda, dogs, and *yes*
to the body's thoughtless crush on the world and
her smile flies open like a sun-flushed dove

and right, I know I talk too much and think
too much about what I'm thinking and not
enough about what I say, and simmer too long

in the crock of myself, which is right where I
get when I get this way and want to say
shut up, Simmerman, just shut up. . . .

Nancy takes me to a coffee shop.

TELL THE TRUTH

Whatever she said in bed to you was a lie,

or else, something she had already said,
in another bed, to somebody else.

Didn't it make you shiver nonetheless,

and blush in the dark like the digital clock?
Whatever she said in bed to you was a lie.

Though meant, perhaps, to draw you closer,

it set you adrift in thought, instead,
to somebody else, in another bed. . . .

Whatever truth there was, was in the numbers

trading places on the face of the clock.
Whatever she said in bed to you was a lie

you already knew by heart. You'd heard it

before, said it yourself, in the dark,
to somebody else, in another bed.

The truth was in the numbers, and the numbers

were disconnected dots. Whatever she said
in bed to you, she was lying, like you,

in another bed with somebody else.

❧❧

OBSESSONNET

I don't want to let this thing I got go
so I'll stow it in a sonnet—that way
I can sew it from line to line like a fuse
while in the soundtrack the baton tap
on the hi-hat or Hook's croc's *tick-tock*
clocks the spark that stalks the dark munitions
warehouse of the heart. The "heart": that hackneyed
valentine of verse (L *versus,* "turn of the plough")

or song or—worse—blithe, bland, commodified
greeting. Jump cut: the real heart is *beating*—
pump made of muscle, rackety clapper
in the body's bell. And the thing's smacking
together its lips like steel and flint; it
wants to blow you a kiss, all to hell.

FIVE ATTENTION DEFICIT DISORDER HAIKU

Fall leaves and Li Po's
poems drifting downstream: slow
boats to China: dreams. . . .

❧❧

Karate: empty
hand. Zen: empty mind. A.D.
—huh? Say what? Again?

❧❧

Count little piggies;
count dwarves, sins, seas, wonders; count
them piggies again.

❧❧

How slippery the

❧❧

PLATONIC

I was writing a poem in which the I in the poem was writing a poem. I wanted the poem the I in the poem was writing to be one with which the I in the poem would be happy. So I thought that if I put in the poem a drug which would make the I in the poem, so long as he took the drug, happy, it would likewise permit the I in the poem to write, by writing naturally, a poem he (and by extension I) would be happy with. . . .

Naturally, I was wrong. Naturally, the I in the poem chose not to take the drug (*I'll figure it out for myself*, he said to himself as, naturally, being I, he would). Or else, being I, he took the drug and didn't write the poem. Or, he took the drug and wrote the poem and was happy with the poem until the drug (which, although a drug in a poem, was, nonetheless, a drug) wore off. . . .

After which the I in the poem was unhappy with the poem in the poem because, although it was not a bad poem and was written naturally while the I in the poem was on the drug in the poem (which is, by extension, this poem), the act of writing a poem in a poem is, well, unnatural. . . .

Already, starved reader of this meager poem, if you've read this far, you've probably guessed where the poem's headed. For in the poem, the reader, albeit a late arrival, is, naturally, I (and, thereby, the I in the poem). And though you and I and the I in poem all want to be happy with the poem, we isn't. . . .

For we see how starved, unnatural, and populous its state. . . .

Ergo the poet's banned from the Republic.

❧❧

Levis

You see, you must descend. . . .

—Larry Levis, "Caravaggio:
Swirl & Vortex"

LEVIS

How deep do you want to go?

There is a lake in the brain
and a hole in the lake and you can take

your time thinking about death.

If you think about it.

Also, there are those who will not acquit. . . .
Which is not

a sadness, really,

but a souvenir of sadness:
a tear inside a thimble

inside a dimple of glass:
a paperweight.

And the hole has a name.

꿍꿍

Souvenir, from the Latin: "come to mind" or
"come to aid" and either way

you can take your time

polishing the splintered desks
in the empty schoolhouse

Memory is custodian to.

Memory: working nights with its cartoon
lunchpail and stained thermos

and closetful of chemicals and brooms

and you know it's true Memory lies
routinely just to stay in practice,

and has no references,

and takes whatever work it can get.

≈≈

Levis is dead and
so I am writing this poem

in the . . . *style* of Levis?,
which is work

akin to performing the labors of Hercules
as a musical,

if you think about it—
that's how puerile and insolent it is

and believe me,
I think about it.

It takes me deeper
and the only work I can get

is shoveling shit in the king's stables,
whistling. . . .

≈≈

Who will come to aid and how
deep do you want to go?

In all the stories of drownings
there are those

who stand by the lake weeping,
wringing their hands and rending their clothes and

those who dive. . . .

You can take your time,

and what comes to the surface
of the mind is blind

and silent. The fish

nibble first at the lips and the eyes.

Dead

is an adjective. It modifies.

It takes whatever work it can get and all
you can do is

take your time. . . .

All you can do is sip your drink and
listen to the *tink*

of ice
skating, slowly,

to the bottom of the glass.

Where it melts into a little lake.
Which evaporates.

Which is the only work it can get.

As souvenir,
you can take the empty bottle home.

❧❧

A bottle is a hole
you can fill.

At birth, they pour you into your name
and when you die. . . ? Out of boredom,

having peeled away the label,
they smash the bottle on the road.

Glass slivers shiver in starlight.

And in the hi-beams of a truck
driving all night the back way

from, say, Riverside to Fresno.
Wherever.

It's lousy work and
takes time

but someone has to move the freight.

❧❧

Which is blind and silent
and beginning to smell a little funny,

but I don't mind.
It helps me remember

how I sat, once, at a desk in a school,

with a poem
praised by my classmates

for its safe, derivative diction
and that smug self-derision

that used to pass for style. . . .

It takes me deeper, to the bottom
of the page, to raise

the remains of his words.

They're a souvenir. Now.
It's the only work they can get:

༄༄

You've written this poem.
Time to move on.

Larry Levis, poet and teacher (1946–1996)

༄༄

Miniatures

If having come so far we shall have
Song

Let it be small enough.

—George Oppen, "Route"

BLACK

I sent some words into the night.
Raven words, they didn't come back.
For all I know they built a nest

of sticks and coal and set about their
own dark business. For all I know
they built a poem and let it fly.

BESTIARY

TURTLE

sucks himself into the cave
of himself and what he does
there we don't know. Flip

him on his back and spin
him like a bottle. Kiss
the girls and make them go.

WOLF

Last I heard I was extinct
around here, a thin yip
of silver like a needle

in the moon: that dead and
distant stone rapacious eye
of the *lupus*: mine on you.

COCK

Someone flips morning's *on* switch and
the barnyard's alit like those refineries
you see if it's late at night and Oklahoma

you're driving through. Why refineries
and why, for Pete's sake, *Oklahoma*? sings
the cock like this: cock-a-doodle-doo.

BULL

Call me Dilemma. Show me
the china. Pin a Y to my
tail and I'll kick your butt.

I'm what you do when you lie
through your pie hole. Fly to
my eye—O, run with me, love!

FOX

Color of dirt and tarnished stone,
gash in the neck of woods I trespass
daily on my way to dead, you have

bled a litter of kits into the lip
of rubble uphill and to the left of
what is yours to claim, mine to say.

CROW

Some days I know what you mean.
I too have screamed like a tarred
and feathered glare of eyes,

black-brained, from a trembling
branch between the dead gods
and the mad kings, *Why?! Why?!*

DUCK

In one gag someone yells *Donald Duck!*
And he does. Then curses in Quack or
Quackanese—transcribed as *!@#%!*#%!!!*—

which translates thus: *Alas!, among us*
who is not like unto a duck?—if not
lucky, then lame, ruptured, dead, fucked.

Comfort and Joy

Comfort

When they shut down the planet, we'll all
be out of work. The good news is: wipe
that smirk off your face will no longer be

part of the job description. I've got a
cousin named Dirk with a wife named
Knife. They'll autograph you for a quid.

Joy

How to employ the emphatic *O*?
It looks like the mouth on one
of those little angels broken

out, plugged in, parked on a window
sill Christmas nights, hosannaing
hymns, or aghast. . . . Hard to know.

TRUTH AND BEAUTY

TRUTH

What we don't know won't hurt us.
Ipso facto, stupid's safe. Which
must be why, through the peephole

of their halo, the Inquisitors saw
to Galileo—so deep in the sleep
of their fear was their faith.

BEAUTY

He looked inside to find Beauty.
Found, instead, a hole. Found,
instead, the red smear where a

heart had been and where, if
anyone cared, there was room
to plant a small animal.

HERE AND THERE

HERE

you are like an X on a map,
that small crucifixion of
location where the treasure

is buried or maybe
that boy whose picture
you saw in the paper.

THERE

is another place where Gravity
does not apply, nor Grief plant
its pennant amid a field of bones,

nor Time climb its one mountain
like a toy locomotive, nor Love
drum its fingers by the phone.

Stop and Go

Stop

is a cop with his hand in the air.
Traffic's a thing like love. Where
is the key to the glove compartment

where the manuals, maps, Fix
-A-Flat, and first aid kit are kept?
Where O where is the glove?

Go

Have you ever slept in a grave of sweat? Have you
ever licked out a womb? I'm no one but I've been
someone you don't want to be and know some things.

One is *go* and *go* is the special served in a bottom
-less cup. The midget umbrella is yours to keep.
Happy hour's over. Drink the fuck up.

FROM THE FAMILY ALBUM

GRANDPA F.

> Here's what I know about
> chicken: *The sweetest meat*
> *is on the back*, they say
>
> he'd say back in the peckish
> thirties and forties and prize
> for the family the rest away.

UNCLE B.

> says: *Everybody's coming out*
> *of doors everywhere. . . . Anyone*
> *who'd do that would have to be*
>
> *stupid. . . . Ninety percent of those*
> *people are dead. . . .* Time's a torn
> ticket. We're watching home movies.

AUNT E.

> One Percocet, one beer and she's my dear
> old girl again—never mind the eye
> that's blind, rod up her spine, kaput gizmo
>
> implant supposed to stem the pain. I fold
> and unfold her walker for her. Take her
> to market. Cry *we, we* all the way home.

GRANDPA S.

I told on in 1983 with his spider
-web kitchen and funhouse house.
What I didn't know, I couldn't say.

Alone and dying, what would you do?
What he did was raise the roof
of his mouth with a thirty-eight.

UNCLE X

just kept getting smaller and smaller,
moved from house to apartment to trailer,
slipped into the magic hat of himself,

disappeared; took years to get to this
mirror this morning and—presto! change-o!—
Welcome home, Uncle X!, I'd say were I here.

AUNT M.

collected dolls instead of babies, mothered
her motherless brothers, was crazy
for the little swatch of garden she scratched

from her yard; nursed seeds to shoots, buds
to blossoms: irises and black-eyed Susans
watched her rockabye her empty arms.

CHILD

I never knew, daughter maybe, there were
two of you torn like worn filigree from
the hem of a party dress no one, now,

shall wear. In the ballroom, a young woman
has turned an ankle and what am I supposed
to say? *Now, now, honey. There. There.*

Two Variations

Little Wing

Too many fingers for music,
not enough eyes to grieve—
I gaze at the grave in the rain

that falls from not enough sky
where fly the strange, sweet wings
of things I'm not permitted to dream. . . .

Are You Experienced?

The boughs of the pines, blazoned with snow
(outside the window, where anything goes),
wag their heads in reproachment of: me?

O say can you see it's really such a mess,
every inch of earth . . . someone sang and then
he was dead of it. Which is, we say: History.

Two Reservations

Rome

This photograph of ____ was snapped
in *Piazza di Spagna*, before the door
of *Casina di Keats*, where Keats and Severn

bore those final, unbearable days
of love and contagion—before the place
was cleansed by fire. Now it's a museum.

Nepal

We can shylock a Sherpa to llama
our luggage. We can badger
a Buddhist to plug in the moon.

We can kiss and enlist for more
lifetimes than Jesus let's eat us
an animal and beat it on home.

Two Visitations

The Zen Mailman

one day leaves jelly beans,
one day a rock, another day
maybe a Milk-Bone or two;

then weeks sneak by of nothing
at all: that's the zen
mailman delivering you.

Winter

has bent the backs of these trees back
nearly in half. Every day the snow's
a little deeper. . . . Another way

the cold white glare of nothing
and everything buried beneath it
rears up to say *Pleased to meet you.*

Two Abnegations

Null

There was nothing I could do
and I did it. There was nothing
I could say and guess what I said.

And the nothing I could change—
you name it—I changed it
into the nothing I'd ever expect.

Contributor's Note

JIM SIMMERMAN's work has appeared in
piñatas, stigmata, canine cantatas,
regattas of refugees scudding like suds.

The recipient of numerous surgeries,
indignities, and a grant from Anonymity,
he is currently Professor of Was.

MINIATURES

SELF-PORTRAIT AS ECHO:

> What can I say?

SELF-PORTRAIT AS MIRROR:

> What are you looking at?

SELF-PORTRAIT AS :

> Go figure.

SELF-PORTRAIT AS SHEEP:

> Lost.

SELF-PORTRAIT AS LOST SHEEP:

> See Luke, 15:4;
> cp. Berryman, "Dream Song 28."

SELF-PORTRAIT AS THE BEGINNING TO SOMEONE ELSE'S DREAM:

> *I'm chasing a monkey that's holding something precious. . . .*

SELF-PORTRAIT AS FRESCO FROM THE SISTINE CHAPEL, CREATION OF ADAM:

> You can't touch the hand of God.

SELF-PORTRAIT AS THE POET FORMERLY KNOWN AS SIMMERMAN:

Obfuscate. Obfuscate.

SELF-PORTRAIT AS DICTIONARY DEFINITION OF OBFUSCATE:

To render indistinct
or dim; dark
-en.

SELF-PORTRAIT AS KNOCK-KNOCK JOKE ENDING WITH A LINE BY TALKING
HEADS:

Knock-knock.
Who's there?
No one.
Same as it ever was.

SELF-PORTRAIT AS ECHO II:

We need to talk.

SELF-PORTRAIT AS A LINE BY RING LARDNER:

Shut up he explained.

SELF-PORTRAIT AS FRESCO FROM THE SISTINE CHAPEL II, LAST JUDGMENT:

In the end,
the artist
as flayed skin.

❧❧

WHITE

Whatever I said, I didn't
mean it. Whatever I meant,
I take it back. I mill

each word; I bleach and
knead and break and eat it.
I wear the crumbs like ash.

American Children

AMERICAN CHILDREN

This time when it comes
it comes all the way,
like a fist to the throat,
only harder;
only this time it comes
from inside,
the way a plane explodes,
and what it takes
to step from puzzle
piece to piece of wreckage
still smoldering
on the lake's calm face,
I wouldn't know.
I wouldn't know
because I'm not in the picture
of the cab and the cop
and the rubbernecks
with their hands
pressed together
like cheap sandwiches
or slung from their pockets
like birds.
Sometimes they *tssk*
and look away,
but the problem is,
they have to look at *something*
and so they look at me.
They think they are looking
through a window,
but because it has rained
the window is streaked,
and all they see,
probably, and a little blurry,
is themselves—
which is all they are, really,

even in a photograph
stalled at the intersection
of America and Time,
where *these things happen*
as we say when
there's nothing to be done
and what I've failed
to notice is the chalk
outline on the asphalt,
so faint already
it looks like a wind,
if a wind can live
in a photograph,
might erase it.
Even to mention it
is a violation
to which I am prepared
to plead guilty
on the day of judgment
assigned me.
Until then, I am
sentenced to witness
what Louis Faurer sentenced
to the foreground,
in black and white,
untitled, in 1949:
a boy in a striped T-shirt.
He's so skinny
he wears his arms
like a straightjacket.
How cold he must be!
—each tooth drilled
into a lip
like an Ice Age.
His eyes are BBs.
I don't know what to say.
I don't know what to say
and that is the problem
of this poem

which is not, in fact,
about a photograph,
but about a woman
outside my office,
weeping in the hall.
She is not engaged
by photography
or art or the leisure class
of language at the moment.
She has lost a child,
that's all.
And although it has
been almost a year,
there's no consoling her,
now.
Time has broken.
This is not mine to claim.
What can be written
has been written already
on a Kleenex I gave her.
Let the wind blow it away.

NOTES

"Monte Vista": George Oppen, *Of Being Numerous* (New York: New Directions, 1967, 1968; awarded the Pulitzer Prize in poetry in 1969). The Band: "The Weight" (J.R. Robertson), "Tears of Rage" (B. Dylan-R. Manuel), "I Shall Be Released" (B. Dylan). Creedence Clearwater Revival: "Suzie Q" (Hawkins-Lewis-Broadwater). "There Is a Mountain" (D. Leitch).

"Neverland": "Never Never Land" by Comden-Green-Styne: *Once you have found your way there / you will never grow old.*

"If Wishes Were Horses": . . . *beggars would ride.*

"Wherever She Goes": *Ride a cockhorse to Banbury Cross / To meet a fine lady upon a white horse. / With rings on her fingers and bells on her toes, / She shall have music wherever she goes.* For Terry.

"Hating the Dog": Thanks to "Princess Jill" for the loan of her title.

"Shatter": Villanelle.

"Pain": *The Crucifixion of St. Andrew*, c. 1609–10. Quotation from Timothy Wilson-Smith's *Caravaggio* (London: Phaidon Press Limited, 1998).

"Jittery": Pantoum in tercets.

"Five Attention Deficit Disorder Haiku": *This little piggy went to market.* . . .

"Platonic": *The Republic*, Book III: . . . *poets and storytellers are wrong about men in the most important matters. They declare that many men are happy though unjust, and wretched although just; that injustice is profitable, if not found out, and justice good for others but plain loss for oneself. Such things we will forbid them to say.* . . .

"Levis": Last lines his.

"Cock": "Oklahoma" by Rodgers-Hammerstein. Matthew 26:75: *And Peter remembered the word of Jesus, which said unto him, Before the cock crow, thou shalt deny me thrice.*

"Aunt E.": . . . *this little piggy cried "wee, wee" all the way home.*

"Little Wing": After the Jimi Hendrix song of the same title.

"Are You Experienced?": After the Hendrix song of the same title. Quotation his, from "1983. . . . (A Merman I Should Turn To Be)."

"The Zen Mailman": A true story.

"Miniatures": Talking Heads quotation from "Once in a Lifetime" (David Byrne & Brian Eno). Ring Lardner quotation from *The Young Immigrunts*, collected in B. Rosmond & H. Morgan (eds.) *Shut Up, He Explained* (New York: Charles Scribner's Sons, 1962).

"American Children": Titled after the book of photographs collected by Susan Kismaric (New York: The Museum of Modern Art, 1980) in which the Faurer photo appears.

❧❧

ACKNOWLEDGMENTS

My thanks to the editors of the following publications, where poems from this collection previously appeared:

Alligator Juniper: "Comfort," "The Eternal City," "Joy," "Null," "Out There," "Wherever She Goes";

The Colorado Review: "Bestiary," "Jittery";

Controlled Burn: "From the Family Album," "Miniatures";

Denver Quarterly: "Nepal," "Rome," "The Zen Mailman";

5 AM: "Paranoid," "Platonic";

The Georgia Review: "American Children," "Leash";

H_NGM_N: "Happy Trails";

Hotel Amerika: "If Wishes Were Horses," "Man in the Moon," "Neverland";

The Iowa Review: "Are You Experienced?," "Beauty," "Go," "Stop," "Truth," "Winter";

Lake Effect: "Hating the Dog";

The Laurel Review: "Monte Vista";

New Letters: "Black," "White";

Poetry Miscellany: "Obsessonnet," "Pain," "Shatter";

The Power of Words—a Diverse Gathering of Acclaimed Authors: "Little Wing";

Prairie Schooner: "Contributor's Note" and "Five Attention Deficit Disorder Haiku" (reprinted from *Prairie Schooner*, volume 75, number 3, by permission of the University of Nebraska Press; copyright 2001 by the

University of Nebraska Press), "Levis" and "Road Music" (reprinted from *Prairie Schooner*, volume 77, number 4, by permission of the University of Nebraska Press; copyright 2003 by the University of Nebraska Press);

The Salt River Review: "Tell the Truth";

Shō: "Here," "There."

"Happy Trails" additionally appeared in *The Collared Peccary*, "Nepal" and "The Zen Mailman" on the *Poetry Daily* Web site, "Crow" on the *Poets against the War* Web site, and "Black" as a broadside from Scattered Cairns Press.

My thanks as well to Northern Arizona University for supporting work on this collection; and to Kevin Barr, Mark Irwin, and Bill Trowbridge, generous early readers of many of these poems.

ABOUT THE AUTHOR

Jim Simmerman is the author of four previous poetry collections: *Home* (Dragon Gate, Inc., 1983), chosen by Raymond Carver as a Pushcart "Writer's Choice" Selection; *Once Out of Nature* (The Galileo Press, Ltd., 1989), a "Best of the Small Presses" feature at the Frankfurt Book Fair; *Moon Go Away, I Don't Love You No More* (Miami U. Press, 1994); and *Kingdom Come* (Miami U. Press, 1999). He is also co-editor, with Joseph Duemer, of *Dog Music: Poetry about Dogs* (St. Martin's Press, 1996). His poems have appeared widely in journals (*Antæus, Georgia Review, North American Review, Ploughshares, Poetry*), anthologies (*The Bread Loaf Anthology of Contemporary American Poetry, The* POETRY *Anthology 1912–2002, Pushcart Prize X: Best of the Small Presses*), and textbooks (*Literature: Reading, Reacting, Writing; Thirteen Ways of Looking for a Poem: A Guide to Writing Poetry; Western Wind: An Introduction to Poetry*); and his poetry writing exercise "Twenty Little Poetry Projects" generated the anthology *Mischief, Caprice, & Other Poetic Strategies* (Red Hen Press, 2004), edited by Terry Wolverton. Jim Simmerman is the recipient of fellowships from the Arizona Commission on the Arts, the Bread Loaf Writers' Conference, the Port Townsend Writers' Conference, the Fine Arts Work Center, the Hawthornden Castle International Retreat for Writers, and the NEA. He is Regents Professor of English at Northern Arizona University and lives in Flagstaff, Arizona.

~~~

BOA EDITIONS, LTD.:
AMERICAN POETS CONTINUUM SERIES

Colophon

American Children, poems by Jim Simmerman,
was set in Monotype Dante with Snell and Futura display types
by Richard Foerster, York Beach, Maine.
The cover design is by Lisa Mauro.
The cover art, "angel 2 graphite drawing" by Lucinda Storms,
is courtesy of the artist.
Manufacturing was by United Graphics, Inc., Mattoon, Illinois.

The publication of this book was made possible, in part,
by the special support of the following individuals:

Alan & Nancy Cameros
Burch & Louise Craig
Susan DeWitt Davie
Suzanne & Peter Durant
Dr. Henry & Beverly French
Dane & Judy Gordon
Kip & Deb Hale
Peter & Robin Hursh
Robert & Willy Hursh
Earl Kage
X.J. Kennedy
Archie & Pat Kutz
Rosemary & Lew Lloyd
Robert & Francie Marx
Dan Meyers
Boo Poulin
Deborah Ronnen
Paul & Andrea Rubery
David W. Ryon
Thomas R. Ward
Pat & Michael Wilder